LEADERSHIP METAFORMATION INSTITUTE

TRANSFORMING THE HEART
TONY STOLTZFUS
PARTICIPANT MANUAL

Copyright © 2013 by Tony Stoltzfus

Published by Coach22 Bookstore LLC
15618 Mule Mountain Parkway, Redding, CA 96001
www.Coach22.com

All Rights reserved. This workbook was created expressly for use as part of the *Transforming the Heart* course from the Leadership Metaformation Institute. No part of this publication may be reproduced in any form without written permission from Tony Stoltzfus.

ISBN-13: 978-1492109556
ISBN-10: 149210955X

Cover Design by Tony Stoltzfus

Some of the anecdotal illustrations in this book are true to life, and are included with the permission of the persons involved. All other illustrations are composites where names and details have been changed. Any resemblance to persons living or dead is coincidental.

Unless otherwise identified, all Scripture quotations in this book are taken from the New American Standard Bible, Copyright © 1960, 1962, 1963, 1968, 1971, 1972, 1973, 1975, 1977, 1995 by The Lockman Foundation. Used by permission.

Scripture quotations denoted "RSV" are taken from the Revised Standard Version of the Bible, copyright 1952 [2nd edition, 1971] by the Division of Christian Education of the National Council of the Churches of Christ in the United States of America. Used by permission. All rights reserved.

Scripture quotations denoted as "MSG" are taken from *The Message*. Copyright 1993, 1994, 1995, 1996, 2000, 2001, 2002. Used by permission of NavPress Publishing Group.

Scripture quotations denoted "NIV" are taken from The Holy Bible, New International Version®, NIV® Copyright © 1973, 1978, 1984, 2011 by Biblica, Inc.®
Used by permission. All rights reserved worldwide.

Also by Tony Stoltzfus
Leadership Coaching: The Disciplines, Skills and Heart of a Christian Coach
Coaching Questions: A Coach's Guide to Powerful Asking Skills
The Calling Journey: Mapping the Stages of a Leader's Life Call
A Leader's Life Purpose Workbook: Calling and Destiny Discovery Tools for Christian Leaders
Christian Life Coaching Handbook: Calling and Destiny Discovery Tools for Christian Life Coaching
Peer Coach Training Facilitator's Guide
Peer Coach Training Workbook

Table of Contents

Chapter 1: Taste of Heaven Journaling 7

Chapter 2: The Metaformation Heart Model 12

Chapter 3: Tools for Working with Desire 48

Chapter 4: beliefs and Identity 60

Chapter 5: tools for Transforming Identity 72

Chapter 6: defining Engaging Cultures 78

Chapter 7: Follow-up Guide 90

© Tony Stoltzfus 2013 | All Rights Reserved

WHAT IS METAFORMATION?

MetaFormation literally means 'the form of formation'. It's looking at how personal transformation actually happens and how it is reproduced. Metaformation pulls aside the curtain of religious assumptions that we carry, to discover Jesus' way of change.

Typically, when we set out to change, we start on the *outside*, leaning on discipline and willpower to alter our behavior. Jesus does the exact opposite: he begins on the *inside*, filling our deepest desires in a way that rewires the soul for right behavior. For Jesus, *changed action is the product of desire fulfilled in relationship with Him*. This 'form of formation'—an inside-out way of change—is as powerful as it is unfamiliar.

The Leadership MetaFormation Institute lets you experience and learn this radically different way of transformation. Since Jesus' method is relational and experiential, so is our training. These innovative courses employ the arts, activations, brain science, live demos, original music, coaching practice, and wave upon wave of God encounters to change the way you change. Then we follow up with the tools and coaching skills you need to walk others through the change process and build organizational cultures of transformation.

It all really comes down to meeting God in our places of brokenness—and discovering that he is good beyond our wildest imagining. So welcome to the God-adventure! Today is a good day to meet a good God—who is always in a good mood!

LMI's Mission

Our mission is to train 100,000 incarnational leaders in 25 years who consistently experience transformation, have the tools to transform others and who build organizational cultures of transformation in every sphere of global society.

Presenter

LMI founder and master coach Tony Stoltzfus carries a life-time of experience in heart transformation and meeting God in any circumstance. He is an international leader in the coaching field, the author of ten books, and has walked with thousands of leaders as they encounter God powerfully in difficult situations. Tony is known for his innovative, experiential training style, eminently practical material and his great heart for people.

"Tony Stoltzfus is one of the most genuine, caring, skilled and helpful people you are ever likely to meet… His passion for each person to experience the healing, empowering love of Jesus is only second only to his own passion to know the Lord himself."

Danny Silk, Bethel Church, Redding, CA

Going Deeper

The MetaFormation model offers a course with a follow-up application process for each of the three main *Gateways to the Heart*. These gateways are the primary channels God uses to speak to us: directly through our *spirit*, through *relationships* and through life *circumstances*. Each course focuses on meeting God personally through a particular gateway, learning the tools for helping others engage, and then building cultures of engaging.

You can register for each course at www.Meta-Formation.com. Come back together with your follow-up team and get a special group discount!

The three courses are:

Transforming the Heart

Our foundational course explores the basic workings of the heart, Jesus' model of change and how to live in a powerful, daily conversation with Jesus at the heart level. Beginning with a 90-minute *Taste of Heaven* encounter, you'll experience deep change and inner renovation in the midst of incredible intimacy and approval—from both God and your teammates. Transforming the Heart uses the arts, brain science, learning games, encounters and more to help you experience transformation and learn the tools for transforming others.

Relating from the Heart

Relational transformation is about allowing God to speak to your heart through others. One of the primary ways God builds us and gets our attention is through hearing words of life from the body of Christ. Covering areas like challenging forward instead of confronting, speaking to blind spots, healthy feedback, speaking words of life, and more, this course will revolutionize your relationships. From the opening *Relationships of Heaven* encounter to the amazing intimacy of the follow-up teams, *Relating from the Heart* will greatly deepen your experience of God through his people.

Living from the Heart

This course explores the third leg of the three ways God speaks to us: through our life circumstances. Beginning with the amazing *Book of Life* encounter, we'll explore how everything that happens to us moves us toward our destiny if we engage it according to God's purposes. Using tools like the calling timeline, we'll dig into your life and find the hand of God all over it, then show how to coach others into finding God in all of life. You'll learn powerful transformational coaching techniques from a master coach who brings God's perspective to difficult situations.

Upcoming Events

For information on upcoming events or hosting an event at your location, visit our website at www.Meta-Formation.com or contact us at Office@Meta-Formation.com.

How to Use this Manual

Adult learning happens best when it includes experience and reflection, not teaching alone. As we work through this material, opportunities to record your thoughts, questions and insights will come on every page. Therefore, we've left the lined pages on the right blank to give you extra space to write. You can use this space for:

- Your own reflections
- To write down questions for the presenter, yourself or God
- To explore emotions, beliefs or desires
- For journaling your thoughts during an exercise or experience
- To log your journey

Our desire is that you will fully engage in the opportunities for personal transformation in this course, learn tools to use in helping others and discover how to seed this way of life into the organizations you lead. Enjoy the journey!

Chapter 1

Taste of Heaven Journaling

Taste of Heaven Journaling

Who was Jesus to you today? How did you meet Him?

What is stirred in you? What emotions are you experiencing?

How did the affirmations and words of encouragement impact you?

What did Jesus say to you?

Where did you resist or experience feeling awkward or uncomfortable?

Where did this experience challenge your beliefs about God and self?

What God is Saying to Me ~

What God is Saying to Me ~

Chapter 2
The MetaFormation Heart Model

The MetaFormation Heart Model

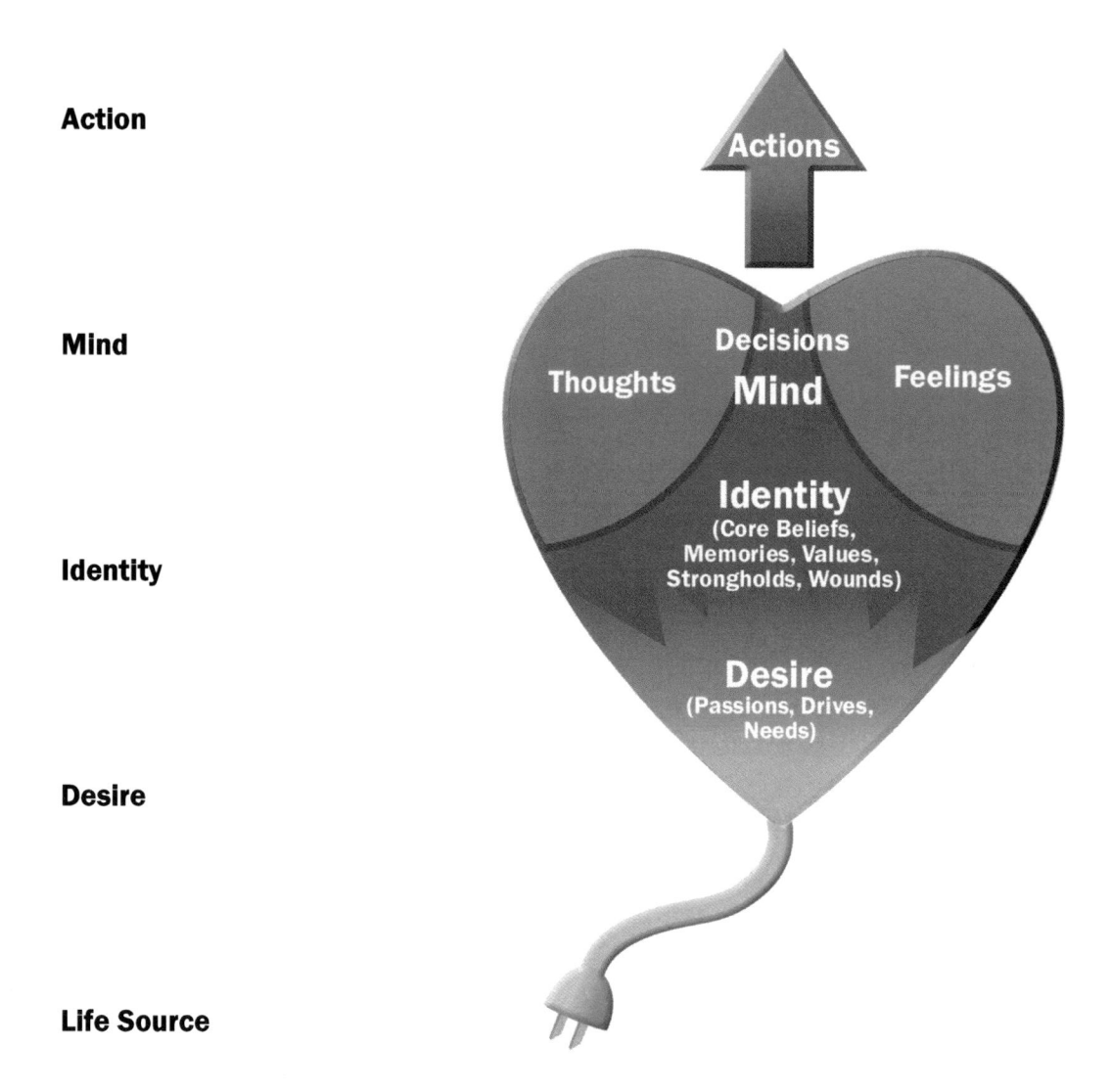

Action

Mind

Identity

Desire

Life Source

© Tony Stoltzfus 2013 | All Rights Reserved

DESIRES
The underlying needs and motivations rooted in my humanness that drive me.

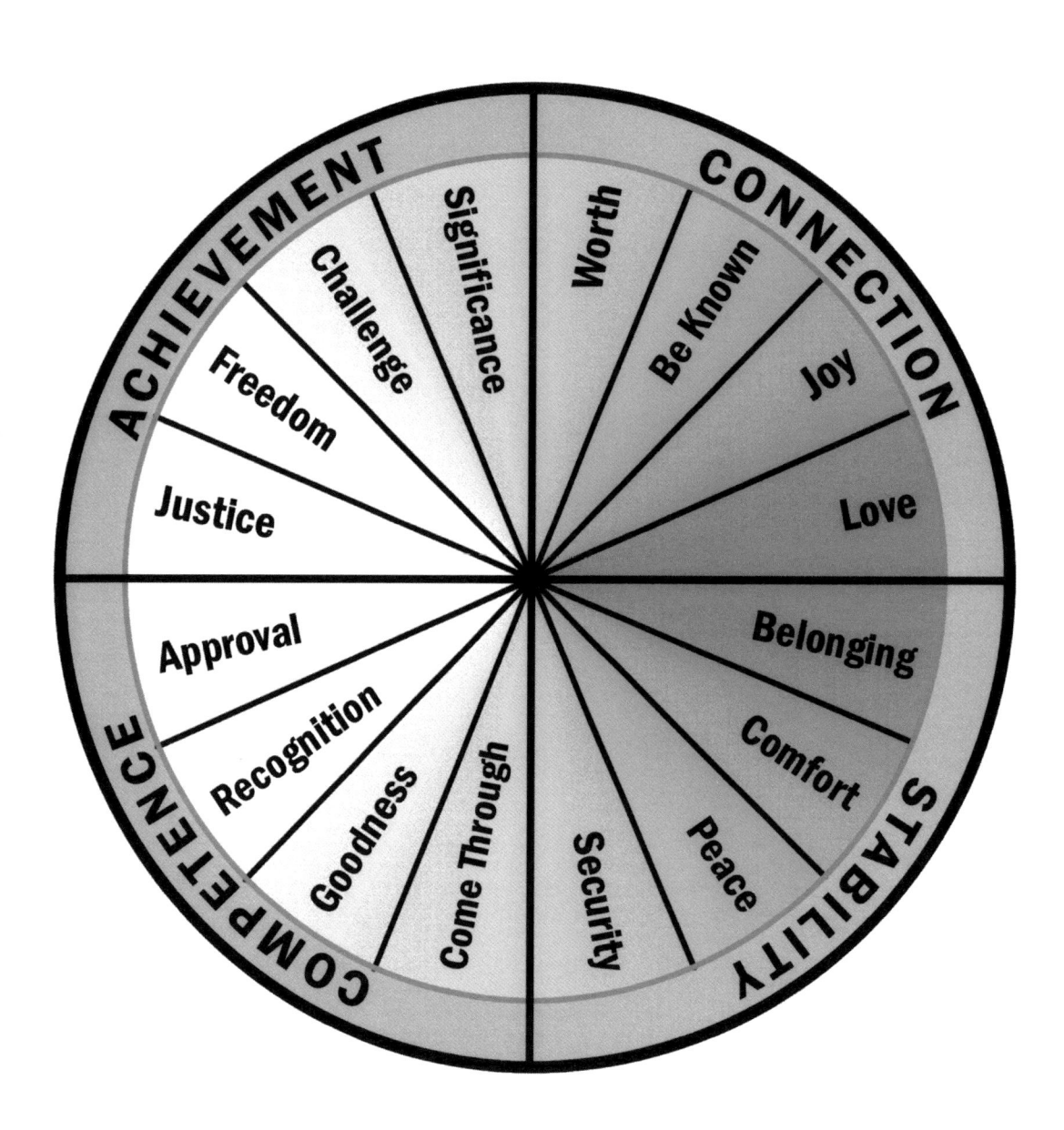

ACHIEVEMENT: Significance, Challenge, Freedom, Justice

CONNECTION: Worth, Be Known, Joy, Love

COMPETENCE: Approval, Recognition, Goodness, Come Through

STABILITY: Security, Peace, Comfort, Belonging

© Tony Stoltzfus 2013 | All Rights Reserved

The Language of Desire

Desire	Related Words	Related Fears
Worth	Value, validity, to be special, respect, honor	Worthless, invalid, dishonored
Know/Be Known	Understand/be understood, validity, be heard, connection	Misunderstood, not heard, unknown
Joy	Happiness, delight, fun, fulfillment, satisfaction,	Unhappiness, pain
Love	Intimacy, to be chosen or delighted in, interdependence, affection, friendship	Rejection
Comfort	Freedom from pain, to be held, to be ministered to	Being bereft
Belonging	Acceptance, relationship, companionship, connection, community, family, friendship	Loneliness, not belonging
Peace	Rest, calm, tranquility, serenity, contentment, letting go, wholeness, completion	Anxiety, fear of pain
Security	Safety, stability, order, to be protected/protect, provision, hope	Being out of control, chaos, not having
To Come Through	Loyal, dependable, faithful, trustworthy	Letting you down
Goodness	To be right, pure, righteous, moral, character, proud of what you've done, have integrity	Failure, being wrong
Recognition	Affirmation, to be special, reward, honor, be seen	Being passed over
Approval	Well done, to be acceptable, acceptance, success, commendation, promotion	Failure, disapproval
Justice	Idealism, fairness, fighting for what's right, heroic	Powerlessness
Freedom	Self-determination, free will, flexibility, choice, be myself, powerful, self-reliance, self-control	Being controlled, loss of opportunity
Significance	Legacy, achievement, changing the world, importance, influence, to be part of something larger, impact	Insignificance. wasted life, being sidelined
Challenge	Purpose, meaning, a goal, risk, excited, conquering something, reaching potential, winning	Monotony, boredom
Physical Needs	Safety (clothing, shelter), nourishment (food, water), air, sleep, sex, exercise/activity	Death, lack

© Tony Stoltzfus 2013 | All Rights Reserved

HUMAN NATURE

Unredeemed Human Nature

"…I see a different law in the members of my body, waging war against the law of my mind and making me a prisoner of the law of sin which is in my members."

Rm. 7:23

Some Twisted Desires

- Fear of rejection
- Fear of failure
- Control
- Fame
- People-pleasing
- Lust
- Greed
- Apathy
- Vengeance
- Envy
- Pride
- Selfishness

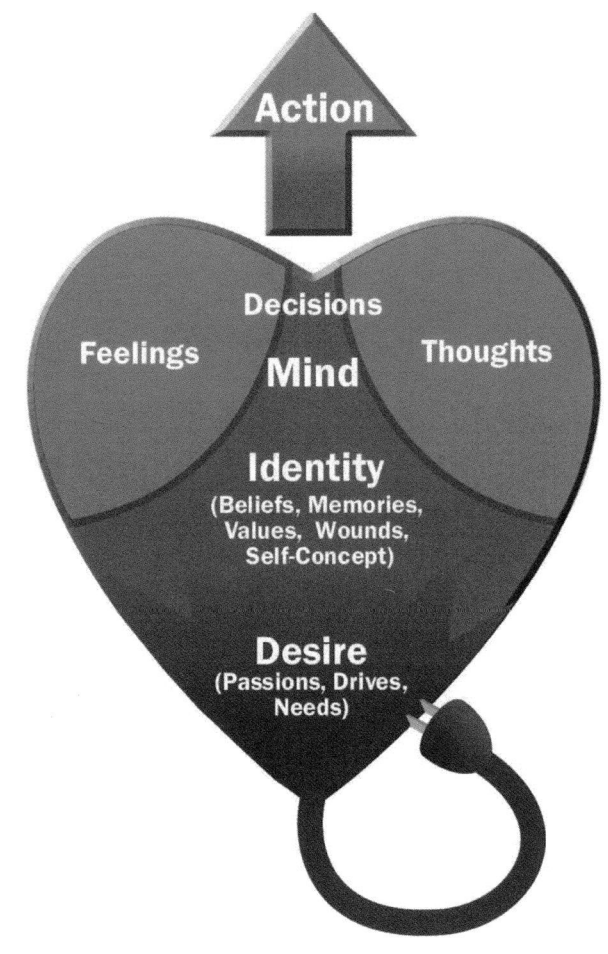

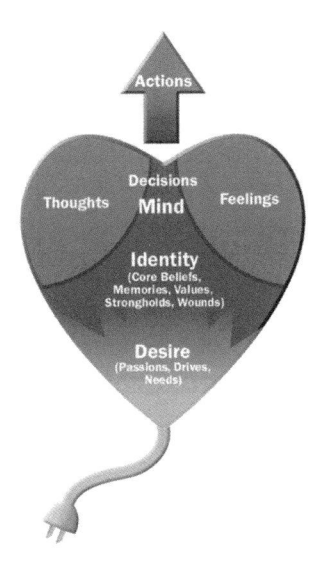

Redeemed Human Nature

- Desires filled in relationship with God
- No longer enslaved to sin
- Life works upward through one's entire being

How the Heart Works

1. **Desire: I have physical and psychological needs that drive me.**
   God created me with these desires. It's part of being human

2. **Desires are designed to be <u>filled</u> within our relationship with God.**

   "Delight yourself in the Lord; and He will give you the desires of your heart" (Ps 37:4).

   "He who believes in Me, as the Scripture said, 'From his innermost being will flow rivers of living water'" (Jn. 7:38).

3. **Experiencing desire fulfilled makes living by Christian principles possible.**
   When desire is fulfilled, I am no longer enslaved to using all the resources of the self to meet my needs and desires.

4. **There is a different change tool for each level of the heart:**

   a. **Desires are filled, not changed**
      Denial and discipline are ineffective in working with desires

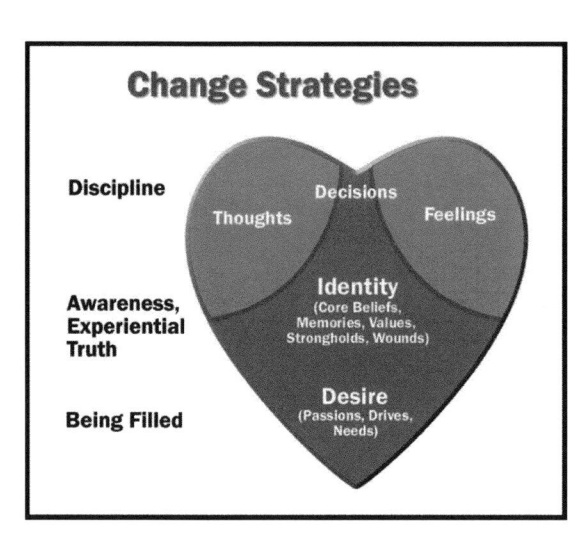

   b. **Experiential truth changes identity**
      Different experiences enable me to let go of the beliefs and identity I've constructed to protect and feed my desires.

   c. **Discipline changes actions**
      When we are free, we act according to our will.

5. **Discipline only works when desire and belief align with our will.**
   Discipline works when the energy that drove my negative behavior is gone.

Forming Teams

Purpose
- To walk this out in real life
- Your support system and brain-trust
- To implement culture building

Structure
During each course week you will:

- Meet weekly for 90 minutes with your team
- Set your own meeting times at your convenience
- Can be virtual (phone with www.FreeConference.com, or Google Hangout or Skype)
- Sessions will be led by a designated facilitator from your team (who will receive free coaching)
- Follow the weekly outlines in the back of your manual

What Makes a Good team?

Choose a Name for Your Team

How Desires Become Twisted

Steps to Producing Twisted Desires

1. I experience unmet desire. That is painful.

2. I decide I must meet my own desire, which leads me to either:

    a. **Fear**
    It twists my desire to a negative. I live out of fear and pain avoidance.

    b. **Hedonism**
    I latch onto a worldly object I believe will fill my desire. I live out of pursuing pleasure.

3. I shape a belief system (identity) to feed/protect/explain that desire.

True Desires Are:

- Pursuing a positive
- Filled in relationship
- Produce an outflow to others

Twisted Desires Are:

- Fleeing a negative (or grasping after something)
- Filled by worldly objects
- Produce an inflow to self

Journaling the Tower Exercise

DISCIPLINING DESIRE?

*"If with Christ you died to the elemental spirits of the universe, why do you live as if you still belonged to the world? Why do you submit to regulations, "Do not handle, Do not taste, Do not touch" (referring to things which all perish as they are used), according to human precepts and doctrines? These have indeed an appearance of wisdom in promoting rigor of devotion and self-abasement and severity to the body, **but they are of no value in checking the indulgence of the flesh.**"*

Colossians 2:20-22 (RSV)

Discipline
…is of no value against twisted desires.

Receiving…
Any other posture twists our desire

Speaking Words of Life

Jesus said to the twelve, "Do you also wish to go away?" Simon Peter answered him, "Lord, to whom shall we go? You have the words of eternal life."

John 6:67-68 (RSV)

Words of Life speak directly to the core desire and fill it.

Rejection/Acceptance
- "Revealing your heart makes me want to get closer."
- "Thank you for the gift of knowing you."

Fear of Failure/Approval
- "You handled that well."
- "Well done, man/woman of God."
- "I admire your ability to look at yourself and see honestly what's there."

Fear of Loss/Security
- "I'll be here for you—just call if you need help."
- "I know you care about me, and that draws me to care for you."

Being Alone/Belonging
- "Thanks for being a part of this group. We are honored to have you."
- "You'll always belong here."
- "Want to come over next week?"

Powerlessness/Freedom
- "You can do it!"
- "Look at all you've accomplished in the past. I don't think this can stop you."

Being Misunderstood/Being Known
- "Can you say that again? It was so valuable I want to capture it all."
- "The more I know you the more I like you."

Fame/Significance
- "Your life already matters a great deal to me."
- "You have a great future."

Worthlessness/Worth
- "You are a jewel."
- "I so value what you bring to this!"

DESIRE AND AWARENESS

Awareness is the First Step in Change

Human Nature Avoids Awareness

"And they heard the sound of the LORD God walking in the garden in the cool of the day, and the man and his wife hid themselves from the presence of the LORD God among the trees of the garden. But the LORD God called to the man, and said to him, "Where are you?"
Gen. 3:8-9 (RSV)

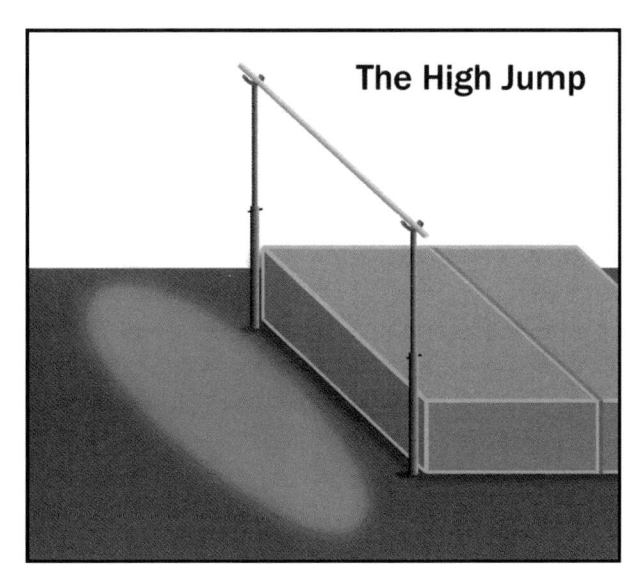

The High Jump

The barrier of pride and fear we must overcome to change

Experiencing Love and Acceptance Allows Us to Look

Heart Transformation Doesn't Happen Easily Outside of Relationship

ROMANS 7:22 – 8:9 A LOOSE PARAPHRASE

For I joyfully agree with God's rules in my mind (my thoughts and will), but there is this law of desire rooted in my humanness that fights back against what my mind wants, and makes me a prisoner of the powerful human craving to get my own needs met, any way I can, at any price.

This inner fight totally messes me up. Who will get my out of this trap: the overpowering inner need that drives me to sacrifice everything I hold dear for temporary relief? Thank you Jesus for doing it! So on my own, without His help, I can try to discipline myself to follow the Godly principles I know lead to life. But my twisted, unmet desires rise out of me like a tsunami and overpower my efforts every time.

This death spiral is swept away for those who have Jesus planted within, because encountering him filling the desires of your heart sets you free from the tyranny of striving to meet those needs yourself. For what outward change through rules and discipline could never accomplish in us (because we're human), God did for us. He sent his Son in the same kind of body we have, with the same human needs and desires, in order to lock up the sin that twists the good desires he put in us and unlock us from the cycle of drivenness that destroys our lives. Now, we meet the requirement of following God's rules without even having to try to do them!

This only works when we leave the old, driven way of chasing our own needs and desires, and have heart-level, relational encounters with the Spirit inside us who is already meeting them. See, people who are caught in the death cycle of meeting their own desires can't do anything but focus all the resources of the self on getting those needs met. On the other hand, those whose desires are met by meeting Jesus are free to just be—to be God's beloved. When your whole focus is bound up in the craving for a love or security or peace you can never attain, all you end up with is death and despair. But when your attention is captured by Jesus speaking to your deepest desires, life overflows with peace and freedom.

When you are in that death cycle of living out of unmet desires, you resist God's rules and you resist coming to God. You really don't *want* to do what God wants, and even when you try, you are completely helpless to do it. Trying to please God by employing your pitiful human will to follow all the "oughts" and "shoulds" your mind serves up is a ludicrous, futile approach.

But you aren't like that. You are learning to live full, out of your ongoing relational encounter with the Spirit in your heart, who fills your desires and enables you to live free. Anyone who doesn't have this Spirit of Jesus present within doesn't belong at the party.

If Jesus has come to live in you, even though you haven't yet thrown off all of the old, dead shell, life is already welling up in your spirit. And the power of Jesus' resurrecting love pulsing through your heart will work upward from desire to belief to mind, eventually transforming every part of the human you into something gloriously divine.

Meeting in the Place of Brokenness

Part I: Become Aware

List as many things as you can that you ought to be doing but aren't:

- What would make you a better Christian or improve your spiritual life?
- How should you be a better spouse, parent, daughter, son or friend?
- What unresolved issues, wounds or sins need to be dealt with in your life?
- What would improve your performance at work, your health, or your legacy?

Part II: Be Present with Your List
- Be in front of God with your list. Look at it with him. Keep it in focus.
- Don't try to fix it. No requests for help, forgiveness or promises to change.
- Become comfortable being with Him in your place of brokenness.

Part III: Meet Jesus
- What do you desire right now? How do you long to be touched?
- Let your desire for peace, acceptance, etc. be filled by Jesus.

Two Pathways in the Brain

The Emotional Pathway

- Faster
- Primal
- Imprecise
- Unfiltered
- Language: image, metaphor, emotion

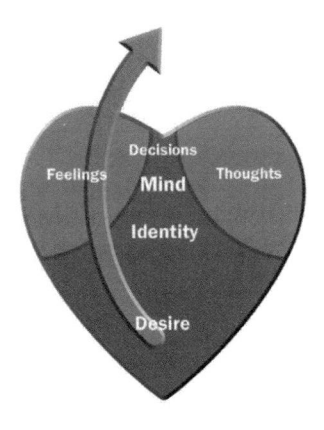

The Rational Pathway

- Slower
- Refined
- Precise
- Filtered
- Language: words and concepts

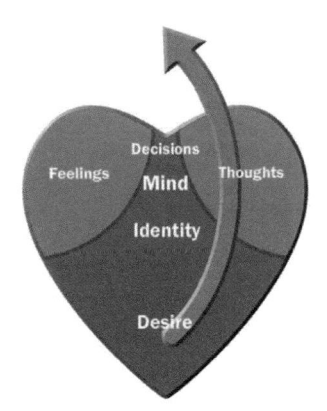

Follow the Emotion to get to the heart.

Rational Questions	Emotion Questions
Ask for summaries, analysis, description, generalizations, actions	Ask the person to re-experience feelings, gut, specific events, reflections, impact
"What do you think?"	*"What do you feel?"*
"What did/will you do about that?"	*"How did that impact you?"*
"What do you do in situations like that?"	*"What happened in that particular situation?"*
"What happened?"	*"What's going on inside you?"*
"What caused that to happen?"	*"Why did that touch you so deeply?"*
"If you were going to write about what you learned, what would you say?"	*"If you were going to create a picture of how this impacted you, what would you paint?"*

Coaching Model of the Heart

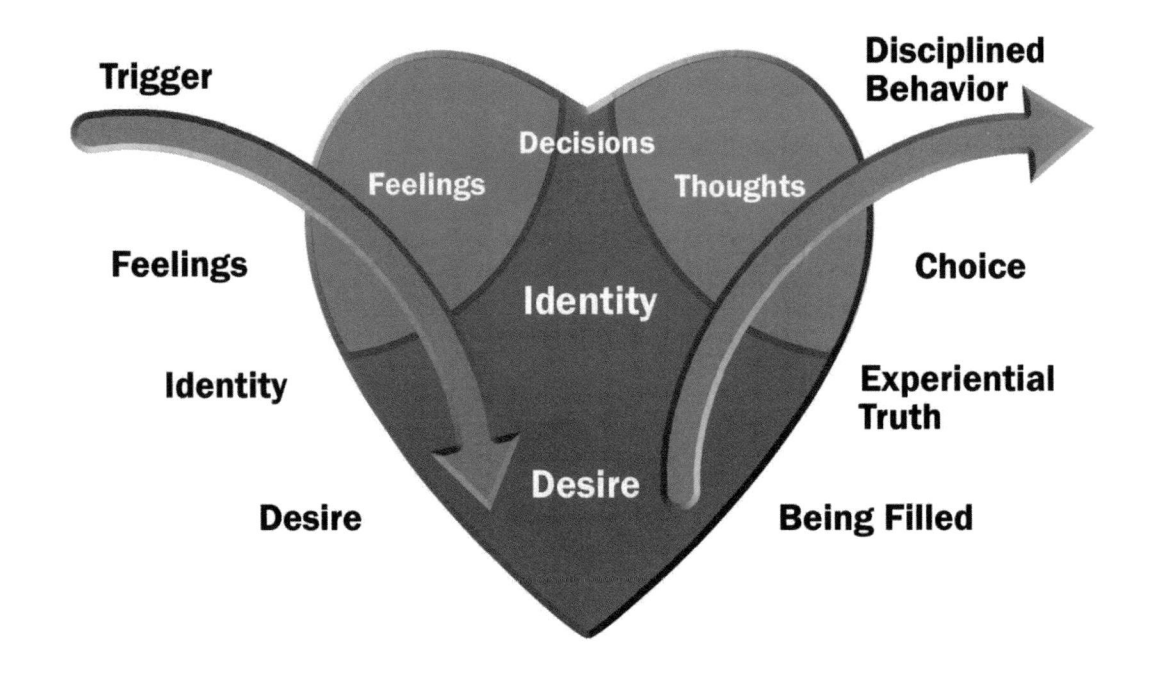

The Rational Filter

Follow the Emotion to Desire

1. Start with an emotion or trigger
2. Explore/experience the emotion
3. Identify your response to the trigger or emotion
4. Ask, "What does that give you?" or "What do you fear if you didn't do that?"

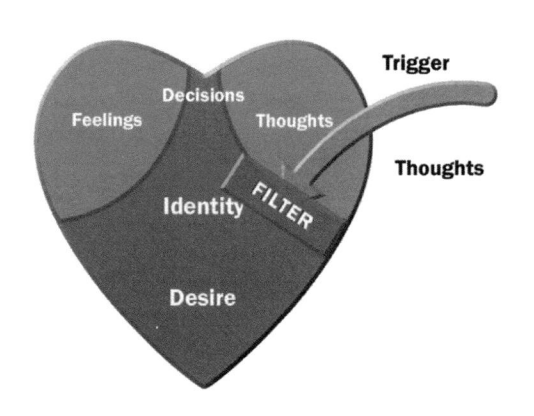

© Tony Stoltzfus 2013 | All Rights Reserved

Negative Emotions

Disconnected
withdrawn, indifferent, apathetic, bored, distant, numb, shut down

Sad
wistful, disappointed, grieved, dejected, discouraged, despairing, crushed

Inadequate
vulnerable, confused, helpless, worn out, powerless, failure, giving up

Unloved
left out, unknown/unheard, ugly, lonely, rejected, worthless, hated

Wrong
chagrinned, ashamed, embarrassed, remorseful, dirty, guilty, broken

Hurt
fragile, offended, wronged, sorrow, heart-broken, victimized, devastated

Afraid
wary, stressed, dread, anxious, threatened, terrified, paralyzed

Angry
resentful, frustrated, annoyed, disgusted, fed up, hostile, enraged

Positive Emotions

Excited
curious, alert, fascinated, inspired, passionate, thrilled, exhilarated

Joyful
pleased, lucky, happy, grateful, festive, satisfied, jubilant

Powerful
adventurous, capable, certain, decisive, confident, courageous, free

Loved
affection, connected, empathy, pursued, tenderness, embraced, cherished

Approved
proud, good, accepted, respected, justified, important, valuable

Safe
comforted, relief, trusting, protected, intimate, secure

Hopeful
patient, encouraged, optimistic, wonder, anticipating, eager, believing

Peaceful
comfortable, at rest, relaxed, content, calm, fulfilled, serene

© Tony Stoltzfus 2013 | All Rights Reserved

COACHING DESIRES UNDER DREAMS

What creates transformation in the realm of desires?

Dreams
"Dreams are desires wrapped in a picture of what we believe will fulfill them."

What is the difference between a dream that fills desire in a healthy way and an idol?

Coaching from Dream to Desire
1. Visualize the dream—experience it

2. Identify/follow the emotion

3. Identify desires with the desire questions

The Desire Questions
- "What does that give you?"
- "What do you fear if you don't do that?"

Chapter 3

Tools for Working with Desire

Desire Tools

Tool #1: Desire Prayers

A desire prayer is a question asking Jesus to touch your core desires. Here are some principles for creating desire prayers. They are:

About the Relationship, not the Business
- About how you love each other instead of performance
- Instead of, "Jesus, help me do…" pray, "Jesus, how have you…?"

From Faith
- Not a desperate plea
- Instead of, "Do you love me?" pray, "How do you love me?"
- Desire prayers assume God is already acting on your behalf

From a Receiving Posture
- About how Jesus is touching us, not what we can accomplish for him
- No performance required

An Experiential Word (Rhema, not Logos)
- An experiential, revelatory encounter with the living God
- We use logos to test rhema, not to substitute for it

A Fresh Word
- Often the prayer is, "How have you touched me today?"
- Immediate and personal, not historical

Examples of Desire Prayers
- *"What do you like about me today?"*
- *"Here are some things I love about you—what do you love about me?"*
- *"What have you been doing to pursue me in the last 24 hours?"*
- *"Here is how I see myself: _____. How do **you** see me?"*
- *"How have you have been my safety and security this week?"*
- *"Who do you want to be to me today?"*
- *"I'm afraid today this won't go well. What do you want to say to my fear?"*
- *"I'd like to do this together with you. What do you want?"*

Types of Desire Prayers

1. Ask Jesus how he sees you or feels about you.
   "Jesus, what do you love about me today?"

2. Ask Jesus to tell you who you are.
   "When I can't finish a project, I feel like I am a failure. Who am I in your eyes?"

3. Ask him to touch your desire.
   "Jesus, I have a deep desire for peace right now. Could you touch me there?"

4. Ask what he has been doing for you that you don't see.
   "Jesus, how have you been pursuing me this week?"

5. Ask how something impacts Jesus' heart.
   "What goes on in you when you see me function in my destiny? How does that impact you?"

6. Tell Jesus how something impacts your heart.
   "Jesus, when you provide unexpectedly, I feel surprised, joyful—it just makes my heart sing."

7. Take a statement in scripture, hear it as spoken to you and soak in it. Let the words sink into your heart.
   "Jesus, I receive that as I come to you, you will give me rest."

8. Give thanks for a statement Jesus makes to you that touches your desire.
   "Thank you for putting me at rest, Jesus. I am really grateful for how you touch me."

9. Ask what things are like when desires are filled in heaven.
   "What will it be like to 'shine like the sun' in Father's kingdom?"

10. Ask for a revelation of who Jesus is.
    "You seem to take special pleasure in blessing the people the world ignores. Tell me about that part of you—I want to know more."

11. Ask what went on in Jesus in a certain situation.
    "When Peter asked for permission to step out of the boat and walk on water with you, what did you experience in that moment? How were you feeling?"

12. Ask Jesus about a feeling he expressed.
    "Jesus, what were you tapping into when you wept over Jerusalem? What did you see?"

13. Ask one member of the Trinity about another.
    "Jesus, when you see the Spirit living in and working through me, what do you love about him?"

14. Identify with the desire of a character in scripture, and receive Jesus' response to that person out of your identification.
    "The woman caught in adultery was terrified. They didn't care about her—they just wanted to use her death to score a political point. I've felt like that. And I love how even though she completely blew it, you put your own life on the line to save her. Thanks for doing that for me."

Tool #2: Speaking Words of Life

Words of Life are when Jesus speaks through the members of his body to fill our deep desires. A word of life targets a particular desire, and:

- Tells the person who they really are
- Points out their glory in that area
- Meets their deep desire in your relationship with them

Desire/Twisted Desire	Example of Speaking to the Desire
Love/being left alone	"I am so grateful that you are my friend."
Acceptance/fear of rejection	"The more I know of you the more I appreciate you. I love that part of you that comes out in these moments."
To do well/fear of failure	"You are doing really well. I am proud of you."
Harmony/fear of conflict	"We may disagree about some things but I am committed to our relationship and I am not going to let go."
Honor/fame	"You matter to me, and to the people around you."
Security/control	"You have so many great examples of God coming through for you—looking at your story gives me confidence that everything is going to be alright."
Significance/fear of wasting my life	"Your life isn't wasted. It was worth it just for your impact on me."
Justice/fear of powerlessness	"Even though a lot of people don't know what went on there, I do—and the courage you showed makes me want to promote you and give you opportunity to replace what you lost."
Worth/fear of rejection	"You are an incredible well of wisdom and life—how valuable!"

Tool #3: The Fellowship of His Sufferings

"...that I may know Him and the power of His resurrection and the fellowship of His sufferings, being conformed to His death; in order that I may attain to the resurrection from the dead."
Phil 3:10

Where or how have I suffered?

What do I share with Jesus?
When did he go through something similar?

- Physical pain
- Betrayal by a close friend
- Being misunderstood
- Being unjustly accused
- Losing your ministry
- Growing up without a father
- Rejection by friends and family
- Death of a loved one

What do Jesus and I have to talk about?
- How did you feel when that happened to you?
- Here's what I experienced—what was it like for you?
- How did you deal with it?
- When Judas kissed you—what was going through your mind?
- How did you handle the pain of losing your dad?
- How did you feel when the disciples feel asleep when you needed them most?
- What was it like when your closest friends couldn't understand who you were?
- Where you ever disappointed? Sad? Lonely?
- How did you feel when your friend John the Baptist was murdered?

Tool #4: Your Glory

*"The Spirit Himself testifies with our spirit that we are children of God, and if children, heirs also, heirs of God and fellow heirs with Christ, if indeed we **suffer** with Him so that we may also be **glorified** with Him. For I consider that the **sufferings** of this present time are not worthy to be compared with the glory that is to be revealed [in] us."*

Rm. 8:16-18

Glory is approval, fame, splendor, honor, brightness, and majesty.

Human glory is often closely connected with suffering in the New Testament.

Glory is the other side of vulnerability. An authentic life is as transparent about its glory as it is about its brokenness.

Your glory is what you have given, sacrificed and suffered for the Kingdom of God, and who you have become through that.

Chapter 4
Beliefs and Identity

Beliefs and Identity

Identify Forms When We:

1. Have a powerful **experience**
2. Assign a **meaning** to it
3. Live out of that **belief** and emotional memory

"Beliefs are about meaning; desires are about motivation."

"Don't make doctrine when you're wounded."

"Much of our pain comes from our beliefs."

Reflections on the Puzzle Game

What emotions are/were you experiencing during the game?

What do you really want to do or say?

What beliefs can you identify that are behind your responses?

Which responses did you have that you didn't understand or can't figure out?

Leading in Engaging Beliefs

1. Awareness is the first step in change. What leads to awareness of beliefs and identity?

2. What in the environment of this workshop made your belief insights possible?

3. How has consistently encountering God in your desires and broken places impacted your ability to look at your beliefs?

4. What does this tell you about how to lead and build cultures of heart engaging?

21 Days of Fun Exercise

	What I Am Adding for Fun	What I Am Cutting to Make Room
1		
2		
3		
4		
5		
6		
7		
8		
9		
10		
11		
12		
13		
14		
15		
16		
17		
18		
19		
20		
21		

Process: Following Emotion to Belief

Step 1: Start with a Trigger or Emotion
An interesting emotion, action or reaction

Step 2: Describe the Feeling
Talk about it, enter into and re-experience it, connect with it

- *"What emotions do you experience when you think of this?"*
- *"Can you name the feeling?"*
- *"Visualize yourself back in that situation. What's going on in you as you do?"*
- *"We're looking for feelings, not thoughts or analysis, because they are a better indicator of what's in your heart. What is the emotion?"*

Step 3: Explore the Rationale behind the Feeling
The belief is in the "why"

- *"Why do you think you felt that way?"*
- *"What led you to do what you did?"*
- *"What beliefs or expectations led to that feeling or response?"*
- *"Frustration comes from expecting something that doesn't happen. What did you expect?"*
- *"How should things work in this kind of situation?"*
- *"What do you believe about yourself and your capabilities here?"*
- *"What does your gut believe about God in this situation?"*

Step 4: Put the Rationale into a Belief Statement
Often, people will say the belief in conversation, and you just have to point it out

- *"So what do you believe in this situation?"*
- *"If you were going to state that belief in a sentence, what would you say?"*

Chapter 5
Tools for Transforming Identity

TOOLS FOR TRANSFORMING IDENTITY

Identity is rooted in powerful experiences we've assigned meaning to. These beliefs yield to experiential truth—to having a different experience.

"You will know [experientially] the truth and the truth will set you free" Jn. 8:32 (NIV)

Tool #1: Inner Healing

1. Start with what hurts
2. Follow the emotion to the negative experience/memory causing pain
3. Meet Jesus there - God encounter
4. Adjust beliefs according to the new experience

Tool #2: Vows
<u>Definition</u>: Identity decisions made out of hurt/unmet desire.

Vow Symptoms

- Emotional reactions
- Irrational beliefs: they make emotional sense but not logical sense
- Negative identity statements
    - ✓ *"We're not a church that goes through the motions..."*
    - ✓ *"I will never be like my father..."*
    - ✓ Defining yourself by what you are against instead of by what you are for.

MORE IDENTITY TOOLS

Tool #3: Declarations
Built on revelation:

- What has God already revealed to you in this area?
- How can your declaration let you relive that revelation again and again?

Tool #4: Dangerous Prayers
Asking for situations that accelerate growth or make God's change agenda clear

- *"God, send me the circumstances I need to see what I need to see."*
- *"Lord, give me chances to practice assertiveness."*
- *"I need a different experience in this area. Would you send me one?"*
- *"Do in me the things I can't do for myself."*
- *"Could you put me in a situation that helps me understand this?"*

Tool #5: Stirring Up the Darkness
Intentionally triggering yourself to gain information about beliefs

1. Start with a fear or trigger
2. Put yourself in a situation that triggers it
3. Observe your responses

Chapter 6
Defining Engaging Cultures

Defining Engaging Cultures

Definition
Culture: The shared values, norms and expectations—the spoken or unspoken rules of conduct—that guide the members of an organization in how they relate and work together.

- **Values:** What is important

- **Beliefs:** How things (ought to) work.

What is an Engaging Culture?
A set of shared values, norms and expectations—the spoken or unspoken rules of conduct—that lead the members of an organization to regularly engage God and others from the heart.

Fear-Based vs. Desire-Based Culture
"If people do a thing because they are afraid, no matter how good that thing is, they are functioning out of the values of hell."

Clash of Cultures

"For fear has to do with punishment, and he who fears is not perfected in love" (I Jn. 4:18, RSV).

Fear-Based Culture	Engaging Culture	Leadership Practice

Characteristics of Engaging Cultures

Characteristics of Engaging Cultures

LEADERSHIP PRACTICES OF ENGAGING CULTURES

"Self-awareness and engagement is the best predictor of salary."
Tim Ferris, Culture Change Consultant

1. **Feedback is honored.**
   Practice: Leaders solicit feedback, implement it and honor those who gave it.

2. **Transparency is protected and encouraged.**
   Practice: Leaders model vulnerability and transparency from the front.

3. **Failure doesn't disqualify you unless you refuse to go there.**
   Practice: Procedures for dealing with failure emphasis engaging as the positive outcome. Failure only leads to disqualification if you won't clean up your mess.

4. **Leaders who engage well receive favor.**
   Practice: Promotion and compensation are connected to the ability to lead others in engaging the heart.

5. **Drivenness is frowned on.**
   Practice: Working too much or regularly exceeding hours called for in your contract is looked at as a problem, not an asset. Leaders work a sane schedule and are accountable for their time.

6. **Identity in Christ is promoted.**
   Practice: Organization has a Sabbatical policy, giving leaders chances to detach their identity from their work. Sabbath keeping is encouraged and modeled as a check on drivenness.

7. **Self-awareness is celebrated.**
   Practice: Leaders regularly display awareness of their brokenness and actively encourage others to do so.

8. **Conflict is seen as a growth opportunity.**
   Practice: Conflicts are expected to be discussed and resolved, and help is provided when resolution is not happening. A good outcome is not when no mistakes are made, but when you grow through the experience.

9. **Suffering is seen as redemptive, not punishment for sin.**
   Practice: Experiences of suffering do not disqualify leaders; rather, those who suffer well are honored. Leaders teach on the redemptive nature of suffering.

10. **Leaders seek out accountability.**
    Practice: Senior leaders pro-actively develop accountability structures to safeguard themselves against power abuses.

© Tony Stoltzfus 2013 | All Rights Reserved

Training Method for Engaging Skills

Tell>Show>Discuss>Do

Training and teaching are different things

"I must decrease, so that they can increase."

"Your discovery is much more powerful than my insight."

Transformation happens best in relationship.

Chapter 7
Follow-up Guide

Action Step Checklist

Before Session 1 Date _____
- ☐ Engage with the Scripture Meditation on Isaiah 53
- ☐ Share your experience with others and how it affected you on a heart level

Before Session 2 Date _____
- ☐ Engage with the Scripture Meditation on Revelation 21:1-4
- ☐ Make notes using the Emotional Words tool

Before Session 3 Date _____
- ☐ Engage with the Scripture Meditation on John 4:1-26
- ☐ Practice asking emotion-based questions according the *Follow the Emotion* technique

Before Session 4 Date _____
- ☐ Engage with the Scripture Meditation on John 11:1-44
- ☐ Speak words of life to others

FREE WEEK
- ☐ Insert a week off at any point before the video conference when you need a break or having a schedule conflict. You have nine weeks to do eight weeks of material.

Before Session 5 Date _____
- ☐ Engage with the Scripture Meditation on Luke 13:1-5
- ☐ Practice coaching around a belief

Before Session 6 Date _____
- ☐ Engage with the Scripture Meditation on Luke 15:11-31
- ☐ Each day this week make the declarations you created and pray the dangerous prayer

Before Session 7 Date _____
- ☐ Engage with the Scripture Meditations from Luke 5:12, Ex 33:18, Ps 84:10, II Chron. 1:10, John 17:20-21
- ☐ Find 5 creative ways to tell Jesus what you love about Him

Before Session 8 (Video Conference Week) Date _____
- ☐ Engage with the Scripture Meditation on Ps 51:1-6
- ☐ Video Conference time and date _____

© Tony Stoltzfus 2013 | All Rights Reserved

Action Step Checklist

Before Session 9 Date _____
- ☐ Engage with the Scripture Meditation on Luke 9:29-56
- ☐ Spend some time starting your culture building plan

Before Session 10 Date _____
- ☐ Engage with the Scripture Meditation on John 13:3-5, 12-17
- ☐ Take one practical step in your culture building plan

Before Session 11 Date _____
- ☐ Engage with the Scripture Meditation on Mt 13:24-48
- ☐ Identify several images or stories and practice telling them

Before Session 12 Date _____
- ☐ Engage with the Scripture Meditation on Mt 16:15-19
- ☐ Create affirmations to give to team members

THE TEAM PROCESS

We leak.

You can have an awesome encounter with Jesus that fills your desire, but that desire needs to be filled over and over again. You can have a different experience that changes a belief, but until thinking that way is ingrained in you, you won't experience the truth's full impact.

The next step in change is to take what you've experienced at the *Transforming the Heart* workshop and build it into your daily life. Since habits form from repeated practice over time, we need to return to what we've learned, repeat the experiences and the lessons, and drive them deeper into our hearts. That's what the team process is about.

How it Works

For 12 weeks, you'll meet for 90 minutes each week as a team to celebrate what God is doing, cheer each other on, practice coaching with each other and share notes on culture building. You can set up your weekly meetings at a time that suits everyone on your team, and they can be virtual (phone or Skype) or in person. A designated facilitator on your team will guide you through the weekly outlines in this manual. Each week you'll also have guided encounters in scripture to do on your own in your personal devotions, and chances to practice the skills you've learned with family and friends.

Each team meeting will start with 30 minutes of sharing and feedback from the previous week's assignment, followed by an hour of skill development exercises. Each week you'll be encouraged to tie the skill into something that's stirred in you or to something applicable in your world.

Your group will have at least one extra week to complete the 12 week follow-up process, to accommodate for holiday and family time. In Week 9, your group meeting will be replaced by an 3-hour video conference on culture building. The video conference gives you some great new material on cultures, plus helps you begin fleshing out a culture-building plan for your leadership sphere.

Team facilitators receive group coaching from the LMI staff—an extra benefit that helps them catalyze your team's experience and lead your group meetings. The schedules will be set at the workshop when we are all together.

Welcome

The *Transforming the Heart* follow-up process is one which you co-design through your team meetings and your own personal pursuit of growth through Scripture meditation, coaching, art, poetry, or whatever helps you connect with God–and helps those around you connect with God–at the life-transforming level of emotion and desire. We hope that you will deeply enjoy and engage with the concepts, the resources, and the discovery of His care for you in body, heart and spirit.

GROUP COVENANT

Transforming the Heart follow-up training gives you the opportunity to internalize and process the principles introduced during the *Transforming the Heart* workshop, with a small team of fellow leaders. You'll start off by reviewing the heart transformation tools used during the workshop, and gradually build toward a consistent lifestyle of using these tools and building an organizational culture of heart transformation.

Since your team's experience depends on what you do, it is important that you make a serious commitment before you agree to begin. Here's exactly what you are committing to:

Team Meetings

- Weekly team sessions of 90 minutes
- Transparency and willingness to participate
- Supporting other group members in their own personal growth goals

Weekly Independent Assignments

- 30 minutes of personal reading, study, and meditation as outlined in this guide
- Using the tools and practices with family and friends, or in your leadership sphere, and being prepared to report back on what you are doing to your team

Suggested Ground Rules for Team Meetings

- One person coaches at a time. Don't try to do three on one!
- Stay in a coaching mode. Don't give advice or tell each other what to do.
- Let Jesus do the ministry. Help the person hear instead of praying for them.
- Practice conversational generosity. Make sure each person gets equal air time and no one dominates.
- Practice loyalty. Speak up if you are hurt or ground rules aren't being followed.
- Use discretion. Protect your teammates' hearts by protecting confidences

I Agree...

"I understand what is expected of me and I'm ready to join the team process wholeheartedly. I'll commit to be available for all team sessions (except for illnesses and emergencies), keep up with the action steps and maintain healthy, open relationships with my team members."

_____   _____
Name   Date

Session One: Connecting with Stories

Scripture Meditation: Isaiah 53: 10-12 (RSV)

"Yet it was the will of the LORD to bruise him; he has put him to grief; when he makes himself an offering for sin, he shall see his offspring, he shall prolong his days; the will of the LORD shall prosper in his hand; he shall see the fruit of the travail of his soul and be satisfied. By his knowledge shall the righteous one, my servant, make many to be accounted righteous; and he shall bear their iniquities.

"Therefore I will divide him a portion with the great, and he shall divide the spoil with the strong; because he poured out his soul to death, and was numbered with the transgressors; yet he bore the sin of many, and made intercession for the transgressors."

Reflection

Use a different reflection question each time you use this scripture in your devotions:

1. Put yourself into the Father's mind frame in verse 10. How does it touch you to see what will happen from his perspective? What does he say to you when you do?

2. There was a first time Jesus read this, a moment when he realized who it was the prophet was talking about. Ask him about that experience: "Jesus, how did you feel the first time you read this passage and realized it was talking about you?"

3. Isaiah says, "He shall see the fruit of the travail of his soul and be satisfied." Pick a place where you have experienced suffering and fellowship with Jesus around it. "Jesus, what is it like for you to experience the fruit of what you suffered? What is the fruit of my travail of soul?"

4. "Jesus, what is it like for you to be dividing a portion with the great? Can you give me a picture of what happened in heaven when you returned? What were you experiencing then?

Action Step

Share what you experienced at the workshop with a friend or loved one this week. See if you can communicate how this touched you on each level of your heart:

- **Desire:** How did your desires come to the surface?
- **Identity:** What beliefs did you encounter?
- **Mind:** What were you thinking and feeling?
- **Action:** What will you do differently because of this experience

SESSION ONE TEAM SESSION

Greeting (5 min)

Check-in (10 min)

- What did you hear from God or how were your desires touched through the scripture meditations on Revelation this week?
- Describe a moment this week when Jesus or someone in his body spoke words of life to your deep desire

Exercise: Life Stories (75 min)

Step 1: Share Your Story

Take up to 15 minutes each to share some of your life story with your team. We aren't looking for the story of your career (the different jobs you've had), your education or where you've lived. What we want is the story of what made you who you are. What are the events in life that most deeply shaped you as a person, and how do they fit together in the overall narrative of your life?

Step 2: Respond

After each story, take a few minutes for each listener to share what impacted you and how it touched your heart. For example:

- *"I admire you for…"*
- *"I got choked up when you said _____, because…"*
- *"What touched me was when you talked about …"*
- *"I was impacted by your courage in how you faced…"*
- *"What I love about your story is…"*

Session Two: Awareness of Emotion

Scripture: Rev. 21:1-4

Reflection

1. Allow yourself to enter into this amazing picture of heaven. What desires in you are touched by it? Share with Jesus what you long for that this picture stirs up.

2. God's desire is for you to belong to heaven, to marry his son and belong to his family, and to take you into his home so you can live with him. Take a moment and speak to God's desire: how do you want to respond to this expression of his heart?

3. This picture of heaven is drawn by a God who is almost unimaginably good. Ask, "Daddy, what can you tell me about you that will help me understand heaven better?"

4. Tell Jesus what you most long to talk to him about when you get to heaven. Then ask him what he desires to talk over with you.

Action Step: Emotion Words

Put this page in a place you will see it, and schedule a reminder to take three minutes each day to tune into your emotions. What strong, unexpected, pleasant or uncomfortable feelings did you experience in the last 24 hours? Refer to the emotion words diagram on page 124 for help pinning down emotions. Record at least two a day—or challenge yourself for more!

SESSION TWO TEAM SESSION

Greeting (5 min)

Check-in (20 min)

- Share from your record of emotions: what strong or surprising emotions did you experience this week?
- What did you hear from God or how were your desires touched through the scripture meditations on Revelation this week?

Exercise: Following the Emotion Practice (15 min. each)

Following the Emotion is one of the most important skills in coaching the heart. Practicing this technique again will increase you confidence and skill as you use it with others.

1. Take one of the strong emotions you shared during the Check-in that you experienced this week, and have **one** of your teammates coach you down to the desires and beliefs under it. Use the *Follow the Emotion* process on pages 40-42.

2. After you are done coaching, give the coach some feedback on how he/she employed emotion questions instead of rational ones (see examples below).

Rational Questions	Emotion Questions
Ask for summaries, analysis, description, generalizations, actions	Ask about feelings, gut, inner world, specific events, reflections
"What do you think?"	*"What do you feel?"*
"What did/will you do about that?"	*"How did that impact you?"*
"What do you do in situations like that?"	*"What happened in that particular situation?"*
"What happened?"	*"What's going on inside you?"*
"What caused that to happen?"	*"Why did that touch you so deeply?"*
"If you were going to write about what you learned, what would you say?"	*"If you were going to create a picture of how this impacted you, what would you paint?"*

Session Three: Jesus in Unmet Desire

Scripture: John 4:1-26 (Jesus and the Woman of Samaria)

Reflection

Use a different reflection question each time you use this scripture in your devotions:

1. Imagine yourself sitting with Jesus beside the well, in the searing midday heat, as he talks with the woman. Ask, "Jesus, how did it feel to be able to offer her living water? How does it feel to be able to offer your presence to me?"

2. John says, 'Jews do not share things in common with Samaritans.' But Jesus made a point to hang around with the kind of people who would give him a bad reputation—people like you. Ask, "Jesus, hanging around with me could give you a bad reputation. Why do you keep doing it?"

3. Think of a heart's desire that is causing you pain because it is unfilled. "Jesus, where have you touched this desire in the last week? And what living water do you have for me here today?"

4. You must have seen something in her. Ask, "Jesus, what drew you to this woman? What desire did you see, and how did you long to meet it?"

Action Step: Following the Emotion

In a conversation with a friend, co-worker or family member this week, practice *Following the Emotion* to desire by asking emotion-based questions and avoiding rational ones.

Session Three Team Session

Greeting (5 min)

Check-in (20 min)

1. Share your experience of using the *Follow the Emotion* technique this week. What especially stirred you or moved you as you did so? Did the conversation go in some surprising directions?

2. What did you hear from God or how were your desires touched through the scripture meditations on John 4 this week?

Exercise: Speaking Life to Twisted Desires (15 min. each)

Identify an experience where you felt frustration, negative emotion or hurt in the last month or so. Then have **one** of your team members coach you for 15 minutes:

- Follow the emotion to desire
- What do you believe will fulfill that desire?
- What do you fear will happen if it's not filled?
- How can you engage God in this situation?
- Take a few minutes for team members to speak to that desire.

Desire/Twisted Desire	Example of Speaking to the Desire
Love/being left alone	*"I am so grateful that you are my friend."*
Acceptance/fear of rejection	*"The more I know of you the more I appreciate you. I love that part of you that comes out in these moments."*
To do well/fear of failure	*"You are doing really well. I am proud of you."*
Harmony/fear of conflict	*"We may disagree about some things but I am committed to our relationship and I am not going to let go."*
Honor/fame	*"You matter to me, and to the people around you."*
Security/control	*"You have so many great examples of God coming through for you—looking at your story gives me confidence that everything is going to be alright."*
Significance/fear of wasting my life	*"Your life isn't wasted. It was worth it just for your impact on me."*

Session Four: Coaching Beliefs

Scripture: John 11:1-44

Reflection

Use a different reflection question each time you use this scripture in your devotions:

1. Jesus' response to Lazarus' illness is "Lazarus will rise" and "this illness does not lead to death." Ask, "Jesus, what happened in you when you met Mary and the others, grieving over Lazarus' death? You saw something they weren't able to see—how did you handle it when they didn't believe you or get who you were?"

2. "Jesus, what did you believe about your Father that gave you the strength to shout 'Lazarus, come out!' to a man who'd been dead four days? No one was with you in that moment—what kept you from folding up and going home?"

3. Jesus came to the tomb when all hope had gone, and he mourned with those who were mourning. Ask Jesus, "Why did you mourn, if you knew he was coming back to life? How do you mourn with me, when you are already bringing unexpected hope into the circumstances I'm still grieving?"

4. "Jesus, what did it feel like for you when Lazarus actually stepped out of the tomb? Did you smile, laugh, nod your head, give thanks—what?"

Action Step: Speaking Words of Life

Find an opportunity in a conversation with a friend, co-worker or family member this week to Speak Words of Life to them. Can you uncover the desires behind disappointments and unmet needs, and bring words that reveal who God is as you touch that desire?

Session Four Team Session

Greeting (5 min)

Check-in (20 min)

1. How did you speak words of life to others this week? What was the outcome of doing it? (If you did not, what is your plan to make that happen in the coming week?)

2. How did you experience Jesus meeting you in places of loss, mourning or loneliness? What did he bring to your heart in those moments?

Exercise: Coaching Beliefs

This exercise gives you a chance to practice helping others identify beliefs. Do the steps listed below:

1. **Identify a Trigger:** An interesting emotion or reaction you've experienced recently.

2. **Describe the Feeling:** Talk about what you experienced, and enter into the emotion

3. **Ask Why** you felt that way. The belief is in the "why."

    - *Why do you think you felt that way?*
    - *What led you to do what you did?*
    - *What's behind that?*
    - *Frustration comes from expecting something that doesn't happen. What did you expect?*
    - *How should things work in this kind of situation?*
    - *What do you believe about yourself and your capabilities here?*
    - *What does your gut believe about God in this situation?*

4. **Create a belief statement.** Often, people will say the belief in conversation, and you just have to point it out. The reason why is the belief.

5. **Ask: "Is this true?"** Give the person a chance to evaluate the belief.

© Tony Stoltzfus 2013 | All Rights Reserved

Session Five: Changing Beliefs

Scripture: Luke 13:1-5

"Now there were some present at that time who told Jesus about the Galileans whose blood Pilate had mixed with their sacrifices. Jesus answered, 'Do you think that these Galileans were worse sinners than all the other Galileans because they suffered this way?

"I tell you, no! But unless you repent, you too will all perish. Or those eighteen who died when the tower in Siloam fell on them—do you think they were more guilty than all the others living in Jerusalem? I tell you, no! But unless you repent, you too will all perish" (NIV).

Reflection

Use a different reflection question each time you use this scripture in your devotions:

1. Think of a time recently when you assumed that something bad happened to you because something was wrong with you. Ask the Holy Spirit to speak to you about that moment through the scripture. What do you believe there? What might you want to change your belief to?

2. Think of several incidents where you've seen bad things happen to others–individuals, organizations, nations—and wondered if that represents judgment. Ask Jesus what he sees when he sees those situations. What belief is his perspective grounded in?

3. "Jesus, when in my life have you stepped in to shield me from the consequences of my actions? What was in your heart toward me when you did that?"

4. "Jesus, why do you send your rain on the just and the unjust? It seems like it would be easier to understand you if we could predict what you would do. Why did you set things up so we are so often not in control?"

Action Step: Beliefs Coaching Practice

Find an opportunity this week to practice coaching around a belief using the steps on page 70. Look for an incident where someone around you is frustrated, stuck or triggered as the starting point.

Session Five Team Session

Greeting (5 min)

Check-in (20 min)

1. How did the belief coaching go? Who did you work with, and what happened?

2. Step back and evaluate: what has changed in your relationship with God in the last six weeks because of your involvement in this course?

Beliefs Exercise (see Chapter Four)

Step 1: Identify a Belief
Take a few minutes on your own and choose a belief that you've discovered you function out of and would like to change. Make it one of those thorny, difficult-to-change ones: a belief about who you are, how life works, who God is, etc. Feel free and use one you came up with last week, or at the workshop.

Then, do the rest of the steps with one team member before moving to the next person.

Step 2: Choose a New Belief
Have your teammates use questions to help you verbalize the belief, then come up with a new belief you would like to replace the old one with.

Step 3: Identify a Corresponding Revelation
Beliefs change through experiential truth—through revelation. What has God revealed to you or what different experiences have you had that you can build your new belief on?

Step 4: Build a Declaration
Next, put that revelation in the form of a declaration. Your declaration should help you remember and reenter the revelation to reinforce the new belief. (Declarations are about appropriating a 'rhema,' not about trying to talk yourself into something.)

Step 5: Dangerous Prayers
Finally, brainstorm ideas for a dangerous prayer you could use to go deeper in this area. How can you ask for a circumstance that will help you change this? How could you lean into situations that would build your faith for this? How could you invite God to intervene? Make sure you come up with one that you can embrace and *want* to try!

During this coming week, pray the dangerous prayer and make the declaration daily.

Session Six: Levels of Engaging

Scripture: Luke 15:11-31

As you read Jesus' parable of the prodigal son this week, consider the levels of engagement offered by each of the characters in the story:

- Vs. 11-12: Not engaging
- Vs. 17-19: Engaging with the head, around justice and worth
- Vs. 22-24: Engaging with the heart, belonging and love
- Vs. 28-30: Engaging with the head, around justice and recognition
- Vs. 31: An invitation to engage with the heart.

Reflection

Read the short article on the levels of engaging on page 124 before doing the reflections below. Use a different reflection question each time you do your devotions:

1. Put yourself into the position of the father in the story. How did each response by his sons impact him? Ask, "Father how are you impacted when we/I engage you in these different ways?"

2. Identify with the prodigal son when he is coming home. How is he feeling about his relationship with his father? "Jesus, what is in your heart toward me when I feel like I've messed up?"

3. Identify with the brother. The father did not get mad at him—he just asked the son to see things from his perspective as a father. "Father, would you show me a piece of your perspective on us kids? How do you see us when we fail?"

4. "Jesus, how can you just welcome people back and open your heart immediately to them after they have betrayed you and turned their back on you? I'm thinking of your response to Peter. How did you do that?"

Action Step: Dangerous Prayers and Declarations

Pray the dangerous prayer and make the declaration you created in your last team meeting each day this week.

Action Step: Stirring up the Darkness

Second, find a place in life where you can be in the position of the father in this parable. Who in your life can you welcome back? Who can you give more trust or favor or relationship than they deserve, or overlook something that is a legitimate issue in your relationship? (Don't pick someone who is actively cold and rejecting your approach). Put yourself into an experience where you treat someone the way the father in the parable did. As you are doing it, ask for Papa's perspective: "Father, help me see this the way you would see it." What is it like to experience yourself in real life as the father in this parable?

© Tony Stoltzfus 2013 | All Rights Reserved

Session Six Team Session

Greeting (5 min)

Check-in (25 min)

1. What happened when you reached out to invite someone home, and intentionally put yourself in the place of the father in Jesus' parable?

2. What strong emotions did that experience trigger in you? If you thought of someone you didn't even want to talk to, what emotions rose in you there?

3. What beliefs and desires are under those emotions?

Exercise I: My Engaging Experiences (55 min)

How can you illustrate the different levels of engaging from your own past experiences? Take a few minutes and review the article on *Levels of Engaging* in the appendix of this document. Then, have each person identify a season of life when God was dealing with you on a major heart issue, and share the story, highlighting the different ways you engaged God along the way. Use the following questions to guide your sharing:

- *What was the heart issue God was addressing?*
- *Why didn't I see it? What kept me from realizing it was my problem?*
- *How did God get my attention? How did I become aware I had a problem?*
- *Did I shift through different levels of engaging as the process went on? How?*
- *How did I engage it from the heart?*

Session Seven: Creative Desire Prayers

Scriptures:

"Lord, if you will, you can make me clean" Luke 5:12 (RSV) – a leper.

"I pray you, show me your glory!" Exodus 33:18 – Moses.

"For a day in your courts is better than a thousand outside" Psalm 84:10a – David.

"Give me wisdom and knowledge, that I may lead this people, for who is able to govern this great people of yours?" II Chronicles 1:10(NIV) – Solomon.

"My prayer is... that all of them may be one, Father, just as you are in me and I am in you. May they also be in us…" John 17:20-21(NIV) – Jesus.

Reflection

These passages are all examples of individuals in scripture praying their desire. Use a different reflection question each time you do your devotions:

1. Choose the prayer that most captures or inspires you today and pray it. What does God say in reply?

2. Take one of the prayers and put yourself into the situation of the scripture character who is praying it. Envision yourself in their circumstances, asking and receiving the thing God gave in answer. Then ask, "Why did you respond that way? What was in your heart toward that person? When have you felt that way about me?"

3. Take one of your own desires and ask for it with the kind of audacity Moses and Solomon displayed. What do you want God to do for you? Then ask him, "How do you like it when I pray this boldly?"

4. Discuss with Father: "You already know what I need, and yet you still want me to ask for it. What do you like about being asked? What does that do for our relationship that is important to you?"

Action Step: Grow Your Prayer Vocabulary

Let's grow your vocabulary for expressing desires. Your mission is to come up with and use 15 creative ways (two a day) to tell Jesus what you love about him this week. They can be creative words, images that express what is in your heart, pieces of music or art, lines of poetry, scripture verses, a dance or movement, passages from a book, a gift, or anything else that gives you a new way of expressing your heart to God. Be crazy and think outside the box—you have nothing to lose and you can't do this wrong! Make a list of what you did to share with your team at your next session.

Session Seven Team Session

Greeting (5 min)

Check-in (20 min)

1. [Briefly] What's the best thing that happened to you this week?
2. Go around the circle several times and share some of the creative ways you came up with to express your heart to God this week.

Exercise: Desire Prayers (60 min)

First, have each person pick out a desire that's on the front burner for them right now. Then go around one person at a time and try to come up with five or more creative prayers for each desire. Have fun and push beyond the run of the mill—use creative adjectives, words you don't normally use in prayer, even slang. Be audacious–step outside the box of how you usually talk to God. Once each person has a list of five, everyone take one of your prayers from the list, take a minute and pray it, and then share with each other what you heard.

If you have extra time, try another round with different desires.

Examples of Creative Desire Prayers

- *"Jesus, what do you want to fist-bump with me on today?"*
- *"I'm thinking of the song, 'You make me want to jump! You make me want to shout!' I feel that way about you sometimes. When do you feel that about me?"*
- *"Sometimes I wonder if my life makes any difference. What do you want to show me when I'm thinking that?"*
- *"What's a good picture in my world of what your peace looks like?"*
- *"If you were going to give me a title, what would it be?"*
- *"What's joy like in heaven?"*
- *"What's a crazy way you love me?"*

SESSION EIGHT: COMFORT IN BROKENNESS

Note:
There is no team session this week! We have a video conference on culture building instead.

Scriptures: Ps 51:1-6 (MSG)

"Generous in love—God, give grace!
Huge in mercy—wipe out my bad record.
Scrub away my guilt, soak out my sins in your laundry.
I know how bad I've been; my sins are staring me down.

"You're the One I've violated, and you've seen it all, seen the full extent of my evil.
You have all the facts before you; whatever you decide about me is fair.
I've been out of step with you for a long time, in the wrong since before I was born.
What you're after is truth from the inside out.
Enter me, then; conceive a new, true life."

Reflection
Feel free to modify the words of these prayers to make them own:

1. Think of a time in life where you've really blown it. Pray David's song about that area of your life. Let yourself soak in the awareness that you are asking for a gift of mercy you don't really deserve, and that he readily gives it. Then ask, 'Father, what do you want me to do when I blow it?" And, "Why is that important to you?"

2. The Holy Spirit is the Comforter (Helper, Advocate) for us in this broken world (Jn. 14:16). Tune again to a place you feel broken; and ask, "Holy Spirit, I want to experience you here as who you are—as the Comforter. What do you love to do for me in my places of brokenness?"

3. David wrote this song after being confronted by Nathan over his affair with Bathsheba. David committed adultery, murdered her husband to cover it up, made his staff complicit in his sin, and denied everything for a year, until after the baby was born. But in this psalm, David doesn't promise to change. Instead, he admits he has a problem and asks God to wipe out his mistakes. Ask, "Jesus am I depending on you well in the places I need to change, or am I trying to do too much on my own?"

4. "Jesus, I'm like David. I have a deep desire for goodness: to do well, to live right, and to be like you. Would you speak a word of life to that desire today?"

Action Step: Relax
Let's take a week off and enjoy the video conference!

BUILDING CULTURES: REVIEW

Definition
Culture: the shared values, norms and expectations—the spoken or unspoken rules of conduct—that guide the members of an organization in how they relate and work together.

- Values: What is important

- Beliefs: How things (ought to) work.

What is a Culture of Engaging?

Qualities that were present at the workshop:

Fear-based vs. Fullness-based

Creating a Culture Building Plan

Step 1: Evaluate the Culture

1. In what arena do you want to work at building an engaging culture?
2. How well does your organization or group engage from the heart now?
3. How is our current culture fear-based? How is it already fullness-based?
4. What are the key obstacles you will face in changing this culture?
5. What is your role, influence or platform to introduce this change? How much real influence do you have over what needs to change?
6. What are your resources? What money, position, stories, people, current crises, etc. can you call on to help the change happen?
7. Who are the key opinion leaders you must influence?

Step 2: Model Key Behaviors

1. What are the key behaviors you need to model?
2. What are the opportunities you have right now to model engaging from the heart?
3. How do you need to change my behavior to reinforce engaging values?
4. What would be most meaningful for the people around me to see me do?

Step 3: Communicate the Culture

1. **The Why:** Why is engaging from the heart important for this organization? Why should they care about doing it?
2. **The Vision:** What happens in the next 1-3 years in the organization if you move this direction? If you don't?
3. **Buy-in:** What do the people you are leading care about now? What will this new direction give them? How can you help them see how the new culture will give them what they desire?
4. **Understanding:** What information do they need to understand the change?
5. **Comprehension:** How can you use showing instead of telling to communicate more effectively?
6. **Retention:** What are the phrases you are going to keep repeating? What key lines need to stick in people's minds

Culture Building Plan (Cont'd)

Step 4: Build a Prototype

1. Who will go with you? Who do you want in your prototype group?
2. For each person: what does this individual desire? How can you tap that desire to help them engage out of fullness instead of fear?
3. How will you demonstrate concrete progress?
4. How can you structure this to demonstrate the culture to the wider group?
5. What skills will you need to train to set the prototype group up for success?

Step 5: Rethink Structures and Rewards

1. What do people do in this culture that gets them promoted, creates favor or generates opportunities?
2. What behaviors get you recognized or affirmed?
3. What qualities does the culture value most in people? Least?
4. What gets you in trouble? What does the culture frown on?
5. What are people afraid of doing? Of being seen as?
6. Where are we rewarding the wrong behavior? How could we change that?

Step 6: Implement the Plan

1. What did we learn from the prototyping experience?
2. What worked that we can repeat? What needs to change this time around?
3. What is different between the prototype group and the larger organization? What do we need to do to address those differences?
4. How can we leverage the prototype group to sell this to the larger organization?
5. Who needs to be on board for this to have the best chance of success?

Evaluating Cultural Rewards

How do cultural reward systems support or undermine engaging from the heart?

	Support	**Undermine**
Transparency	People are rewarded with respect for transparency and openness. Having a problem is not a mark against you.	You are rewarded for looking like you have it together. We don't talk about personal issues. Transparency results in disrespect or gossip.
Relational depth	People are used to deep conversations and welcome them. People ask deep questions regularly and know how to listen	We talk about sports, the weather and the kids. There is an invisible barrier to talking about our dreams, disappointments or feelings.
Honesty	Honest feedback is requested and well-received. Those who are forthright are respected and promoted.	Everyone knows not to tell certain individuals what they really think. Honest feedback results in retaliation or loss of favor and influence.
Self-Awareness	Aware of your own weaknesses, able to talk about them and to bring others around you to complement you is valued as a strength.	The culture loves people who can do it all. Showing weakness is being weak.
Accountability	Leaders are aware they could go wrong and build accountability structures in their life to help them live the way they want	Leaders are not accountable or actively hide their lives from others. They cultivate the view that they are above that.
Drivenness	You aren't expected to come in early and stay late. People have lives outside of work. Drivenness is confronted, not honored.	Drivenness is rewarded. Leaders lead unbalanced lives and expect others to do the same. Saying "No" is just not done.
Relational Skills	Maintaining good relationships with peers is important. Those who destroy relationships don't last long. Accounts are short.	If you perform, you get the perks, no matter how you treat people. If you are a star performer you can get away with murder.
Character Issues	It is normal and expected to get feedback on your blind spots. Problems won't get you fired—just refusing to deal with them.	We tiptoe around each other's issues and don't go there. Challenging others' personal habits is frowned on or avoided.
Conflict	The culture expects people to deal with conflict. If you talk to a third party about a conflict, you will be encouraged to go to the source. Mediation is part of the culture. Simply avoiding things is frowned on and eventually confronted.	The person with the most power wins. Lower level individuals find confrontation too scary to attempt. Those who speak up are told not to rock the boat. When you are hurt, the culture tells you to just suck it up and keep going.
Job Evaluation	You are evaluated on your impact on people, personal growth and results. Great results alone won't get you promoted.	You are evaluated on tasks and results (if you are evaluated at all). Hiring and firing is an opaque process.
Control and Insecure Leadership	Your co-workers, reports and your boss are all giving you feedback about it. You are expected to change.	Working with jerks is just a given. Hopefully we'll get good people in here, because we can't change them.
Suffering	Those who suffer well are respected for their courage. No one tries to tell you you are suffering because of sin in your life. Everyone expects that you'll find something beautiful within it.	Suffering is evidence that you did something wrong somewhere. People who suffer have a communicable disease — you don't want to get too close.

© Tony Stoltzfus 2013 | All Rights Reserved

Changing Cultural Rewards

"Beliefs change when people have different experiences."

1. Create different experiences through modeling new behaviors in personal or group interactions
2. Directly address the reward system and define a new one
3. Publicly honor/favor/recognize those who embrace the new behaviors. Ask the group to participate in honoring them.
4. Train/teach on why you are rewarding what you are rewarding
5. Pre-empt wrong responses and behaviors
6. Make allies out of your obstacles
7. Change what gets someone promoted or leads to a raise

Session Nine: Culture Building

Scripture: Luke 9:29-36, 46-56 (RSV)

"And as he was praying, the appearance of his countenance was altered, and his raiment became dazzling white. And behold, two men talked with him, Moses and Elijah, who appeared in glory and spoke of his departure, which he was to accomplish at Jerusalem. Now Peter and those who were with him were heavy with sleep, and when they wakened they saw his glory and the two men who stood with him. And as the men were parting from him, Peter said to Jesus, "Master, it is well that we are here; let us make three booths, one for you and one for Moses and one for Elijah"—not knowing what he said.

As he said this, a cloud came and overshadowed them; and they were afraid as they entered the cloud. And a voice came out of the cloud, saying, "This is my Son, my Chosen; listen to him!" And when the voice had spoken, Jesus was found alone. And they kept silence and told no one in those days anything of what they had seen...

And an argument arose among them as to which of them was the greatest. But when Jesus perceived the thought of their hearts, he took a child and put him by his side, and said to them, "Whoever receives this child in my name receives me, and whoever receives me receives him who sent me; for he who is least among you all is the one who is great."

John answered, "Master, we saw a man casting out demons in your name, and we forbade him, because he does not follow with us." But Jesus said to him, "Do not forbid him; for he that is not against you is for you."

When the days drew near for him to be received up, he set his face to go to Jerusalem. And he sent messengers ahead of him, who went and entered a village of the Samaritans, to make ready for him; but the people would not receive him, because his face was set toward Jerusalem. And when his disciples James and John saw it, they said, "Lord, do you want us to bid fire come down from heaven and consume them?" But he turned and rebuked them. And they went on to another village.

Reflection

What is striking about this passage is the culture Jesus built with his disciples. They felt free to speak their minds, give feedback to or even disagree with the Son of God! They seem totally comfortable saying whatever they think around him, and even saying dumb things does leave them felling shut down or disqualified. Use a different prayer each day (or make your own) to explore the culture Jesus created with his friends.

1. *"Jesus, why was it important to you to let the disciples speak their minds? Do you like it when I do that? How come?"*

2. *"Jesus, some of what I've got to say must sound kind of dumb to you, since I don't have the perspective of heaven. What do you hear when I say something off base?"*

3. *"What do you think: am I being too cautious in how I talk to you? What do you want to hear more of?"*

4. *"Jesus, what is your dream for our relationship?"*

Action Step: Flesh out Your Culture Plan

Spend 45 minutes fleshing out your culture building plan (see the "Creating a Culture Building Plan" on pages 112-113) so that you have a good idea what your first actions will be in each of the six steps.

© Tony Stoltzfus 2013 | All Rights Reserved

Session Nine Team Session

Greeting (5 min)

Check-in (20 min)

1. What is one significant thing that's going on in your life now that you'd like your team to know about?

2. Discuss what you heard from Jesus as you prayed over the scripture this week. What is Jesus saying to you about your comfort level with him?

Exercise: Culture Building Plans (60 min)

Have one person share his/her culture building plan in one minute. Then have a teammate coach you through some of the questions on steps one to three of the "Creating a Culture Building Plan" on pages 112-113. Focus the coaching time on the places where your plan has 'holes' rather than just recounting what you've already thought through. Coaches may want to start with a question like, "Which part of the plan would be most helpful to focus on for the next 15 minutes?"

Split up the time so you each get a chance to focus on your own plan.

Session Ten: Modeling

Scripture: John 13:3-5, 12-17 (MSG)
"Jesus knew that the Father had put him in complete charge of everything, that he came from God and was on his way back to God. So he got up from the supper table, set aside his robe, and put on an apron. Then he poured water into a basin and began to wash the feet of the disciples, drying them with his apron...

"After he had finished washing their feet, he took his robe, put it back on, and went back to his place at the table. Then he said, "Do you understand what I have done to you? You address me as 'Teacher' and 'Master,' and rightly so. That is what I am. So if I, the Master and Teacher, washed your feet, you must now wash each other's feet. I've laid down a pattern for you. What I've done, you do. I'm only pointing out the obvious. A servant is not ranked above his master; an employee doesn't give orders to the employer. If you understand what I'm telling you, act like it—and live a blessed life."

Reflection
Use a different one of these prayers each day (or make your own) to explore how Jesus modeled servanthood:

1. "Jesus, the idea that a king like you comes as a servant is hard to understand. Can you show me how you have come to serve me in the last week?"

2. "What were you feeling toward your disciples in the moment when you washed their feet? What did you experience when you washed Judas' feet?"

3. "I'd like to let you serve someone else through me today, and share that experience with you. Who could we touch today with that kind of love?"

4. "Jesus, how can I let you wash my feet today?"

Action Step: Take the First Step
What concrete step can you take this week to model or communicate the new culture? Take one practical step you created in your culture building plan.

Session Ten Team Session

Greeting (5 min)

Check-in (20 min)

1. What emotions do you experience when you are working on your culture building plan? Are you excited, discouraged, energized, overwhelmed—or what?

2. Share about how you modeled engaging the heart this week and how it went.

Exercise: Tuning into Desire (60 min)

Since culture change works on deeply-held beliefs and desires, implementing it is going to tend to stir things up inside us. That's a good chance to practice our engaging skills!

Step I: Identify Emotion
Identify an area of this process where you have strong feelings. Is there a particular person, obstacle to change or behavior that gets your goat? What about the old culture really bothers you? Does this trigger any fears or insecurities about your own leadership abilities? Where are you reacting instead of responding?

Step II: Coach through Emotion to Desire
Have one of your teammates coach you to follow the emotion down to desire:

1. Describe the emotion. Tune into it.
2. Why do you feel that way? What do you believe about the situation that produces those emotions?
3. What is the desire or twisted desire that drives this? What would changing this give you? What do you fear if it never changes?

Step III: Meet Jesus
Take a minute to pray and ask Jesus to speak to the desire. Experience him filling it.

© Tony Stoltzfus 2013 | All Rights Reserved

Session Eleven: Communicating

Scripture: Mt 13:24-48 (RSV)

"The kingdom of heaven may be compared to a man who sowed good seed in his field; but while men were sleeping, his enemy came and sowed weeds among the wheat, and went away…"

"…The kingdom of heaven is like a grain of mustard seed which a man took and sowed in his field; it is the smallest of all seeds, but when it has grown it is the greatest of shrubs and becomes a tree, so that the birds of the air come and make nests in its branches."

"…The kingdom of heaven is like leaven which a woman took and hid in three measures of flour, till it was all leavened."

"The kingdom of heaven is like treasure hidden in a field, which a man found and covered up; then in his joy he goes and sells all that he has and buys that field."

"Again, the kingdom of heaven is like a merchant in search of fine pearls, who, on finding one pearl of great value, went and sold all that he had and bought it."

"Again, the kingdom of heaven is like a net which was thrown into the sea and gathered fish of every kind; when it was full, men drew it ashore and sat down and sorted the good into vessels but threw away the bad."

Reflection

Use a different prayer each day to tune into the Kingdom-of-Heaven culture, Jesus is communicating:

1. "Jesus, these images are from a different time, and it is hard to relate to things I don't experience in my daily life. Can you reinterpret them for me? If you were saying those verses just to me, what examples would you use?"
2. "Jesus, what was it like for you to try to communicate the reality of heaven to people who for the most part just didn't understand? How did you keep from getting discouraged?"
3. "You are the pearl of great price, Jesus. Here are five things I gave up so I could have more of you…"
4. "Two of these images have to do with gathering up the bad with the good and sorting it our later. I'm not sure I understand: could you tell me more about that?"

Action Step:

In these verses, Jesus is communicating the new culture he is building: the Kingdom-of-Heaven culture. He employs a variety of images in succession to help his listeners tune in to what he was talking about—images from their daily lives that they can visualize and relate to.

What images or metaphors can you use to communicate the new culture you want to build? And what stories will you tell to illustrate it? Identify several images or stories and practice telling them in a way that highlights the key parts of the culture you want to build.

Session Eleven Team Session

Greeting (5 min)

Check-in (20 min)

1. What is the biggest personal challenge you face right now?
2. Respond to what your team members share. What do you believe about them and their abilities to face this challenge? What is the greatness you see in them in this situation?

Exercise: Culture Communication (60 min)

Use your team to try out the culture-building stories and images you came up with. While we can all tell stories, telling them to illustrate an unfamiliar concept requires some added thought and practice. This is your chance to get your communication down before you try it live!

One at a time, share them with your team, as if your teammates were people in your organization you wanted to 'sell' on the new culture. Give them a good pitch!

Teammates, give some specific feedback:

- **Communicate:** How well do these stories and word-pictures help you grasp the culture? What is your takeaway from a certain story—what did you learn from it?
- **Focus:** Does the way it was told focus you on an aspect of the culture, or does it just feel like a disconnected anecdote?
- **Sell:** Does this story explain how the culture might benefit me?
- **Motivate:** Do the images connect with me? Can I relate to them, and do they touch me on the level of emotion and passion, or just head?
- What did this person communicate well? What could they do to improve?

If you have extra time, try your pitch again, incorporating the feedback you got the first time around.

Session Twelve: Where Do We Go from Here?

Scripture: Mt. 16:15-19 (MSG)

He pressed them, "And how about you? Who do you say I am?"

Simon Peter said, "You're the Christ, the Messiah, the Son of the living God."

Jesus came back, "God bless you, Simon, son of Jonah! You didn't get that answer out of books or from teachers. My Father in heaven, God himself, let you in on this secret of who I really am. And now I'm going to tell you who you are, really are. You are Peter, a rock. This is the rock on which I will put together my church, a church so expansive with energy that not even the gates of hell will be able to keep it out.

"And that's not all. You will have complete and free access to God's kingdom, keys to open any and every door: no more barriers between heaven and earth, earth and heaven. A yes on earth is yes in heaven. A no on earth is no in heaven."

Reflection

Use a different prayer each day to explore how Jesus built a culture where people spoke to each other's true identity.

1. "Jesus, I love that you told Peter who he really was. Can you tell me who I really am in your eyes?"
2. Make Peter's confession in your own words—tell Jesus who he really is to you.
3. Make Peter's confession in your own words, and then absorb the response Jesus gave to Peter as one given straight to you. "Jesus, how do you see me as a rock?"
4. Take the last verse (verse 19) and absorb it as something Jesus is speaking personally to you—that you have complete and free access to God's Kingdom. "Jesus, help me understand this gift. What are you giving to me here?"

Action Step:

We've come to the end of the 12 weeks of team sessions! Let's end on a high note, by creating powerful affirmations to give to your team members at your next session.

- What do you believe about their destiny and their abilities?
- What can you name about who they really are?
- How can you speak to the deep desires they've identified over the last 12 weeks?

Create several affirmations for each person (see pages 32 and 54 for examples of affirming the heart). You may want to type them out so you can send them to the person after your team meeting.

Session Twelve Team Session

Greeting (5 min)

Check-in (10 min)

1. How has Jesus been real to you this week?

Exercise: Circle of Blessing (50 min)

Choose one person at a time to receive affirmation, then go around the circle and share your powerful affirmations. When one team member has finished giving his/her affirmations, ask the person being affirmed, "How did that impact you?" and give him/her time to respond. Respond out of your emotions and desires instead of your head—and coach each other to do so if needed!

Exercise: Designing Our Team's Future (20 min)

Since the formal part of the course is over, you get to decide your team's future. You could:

- Continue to meet as you are now.
- Keep in touch as friends but stop formally meeting
- Sign up for the next course together (and get the team discount!)
- Or whatever else you can come up with!

Whatever you choose, operate out of your desires: don't do anything out of a sense of obligation or guilt! If you do decided to keep meeting as a team, you'll need to:

- Designate a leader to keep you on track
- Decide what you value about the group and what you want to keep doing together
- Get the dates for the next series of meetings in your calendars

Once you have decided, please send your LMI coach an e-mail to let us know what you chose!

Levels of Engaging

Not every opportunity to engage from the heart comes to fruition. Sometimes we only engage with our heads, sometimes we are unaware of what God is doing, and sometimes we are actively resisting the process. Becoming aware of what different levels of engaging look like is a valuable tool in responding more deeply to God's processing.

Not Engaging

Sometimes, we simply don't see that God is dealing with us. Lacking awareness can be a normal part of the process of God progressively getting our attention, or we can be actively ignoring the situation: refusing to look, lest we see something painful. Because awareness and pain are connected in the brain; we sometimes develop highly tuned abilities to block a thing out. Or, we may deny that there's a problem even when it is apparent to everyone around us. The energy in our denials is a sign that we 'doth protest too much,' as Shakespeare put it.

A small step further is acknowledging the problem but externalizing the blame. 'It was my co-workers' fault, it was the teacher's fault, it was the fault of circumstances, it wasn't fair to expect this'—anything to avoid admitting I have a problem. We blame-shift when we aren't comfortable in the place of brokenness: when being wrong is so scary that we can't go there.

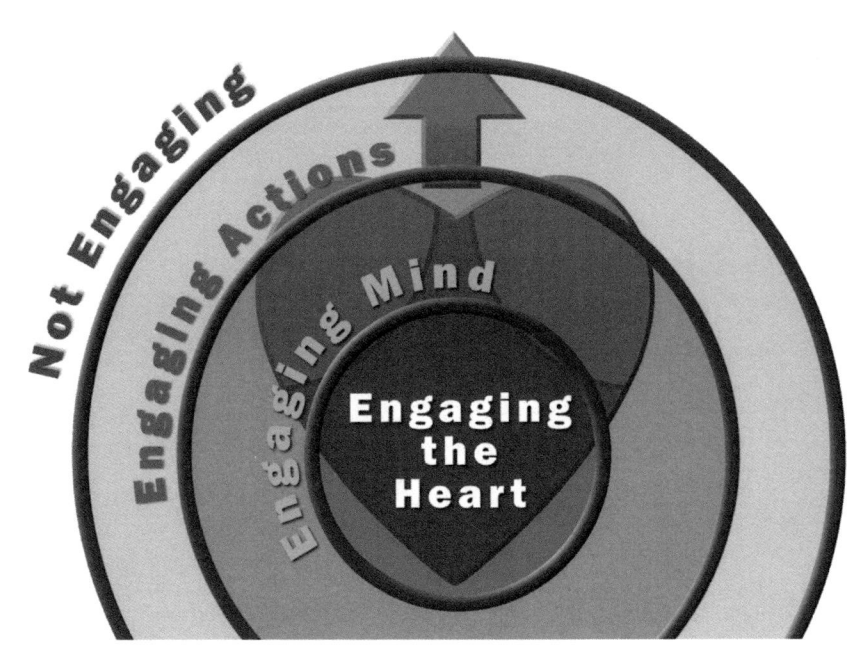

Another form of failing to engaging is to endure without reflection. It is easy to think we are taking up our cross and engaging well, when in reality our only strategy is to slog on and hope the situation goes away without ever doing the hard work of looking at why we are in it in the first place. When I hear the classic statement, "God is just teaching me patience," I've begun to think that 'those whom God is teaching patience aren't learning anything.'

Head Engaging

Engaging with our heads is engaging at a tactical level. We make adjustments, learn principles we can apply next time, examine our strategies—but without delving into the heart that produced them. When we say, "Next time I will do such and such differently," we are engaging with our heads. If someone didn't "hear my heart," and I work on learning better communication skills, that's head engaging. Head engaging is right and necessary—it just leaves much more the table.

Heart Engaging

Heart engaging asks, "What inside of me produced these actions and responses?" For instance, if I feel someone didn't hear my heart, am I willing to examine the possibility that maybe they did—and I'm the one who doesn't know my own heart? If the choice I made was wrong, what desire drove that choice? If I didn't see, what beliefs kept me from seeing? Engaging the heart accepts that at least part of the problem is probably inside me, and is willing to take the risk of seeing the truth and dealing with it.

More than Conquerors

Ever wondered what it means in scripture to be "more than a conqueror?" How can you do more in a contest than totally defeat your foe? Just this—you can win a victory for many others as well. Sometimes the pain of growth and change isn't just for you—it is for all those you will touch because you went there and met God profoundly.

Negative Emotions

Disconnected
withdrawn, indifferent, apathetic, bored, distant, numb, shut down

Sad
wistful, disappointed, grieved, dejected, discouraged, despairing, crushed

Inadequate
vulnerable, confused, helpless, worn out, powerless, failure, giving up

Unloved
left out, unknown/unheard, ugly, lonely, rejected, worthless, hated

Wrong
chagrinned, embarrassed, ashamed, remorseful, dirty, guilty, broken

Hurt
fragile, offended, wronged, sorrow, heart-broken, victimized, devastated

Afraid
wary, stressed, dread, anxious, threatened, terrified, paralyzed

Angry
resentful, frustrated, annoyed, disgusted, fed up, hostile, enraged

Positive Emotions

Excited
curious, alert, fascinated, inspired, passionate, thrilled, exhilarated

Joyful
pleased, lucky, happy, grateful, festive, jubilant, satisfied

Powerful
adventurous, capable, certain, decisive, confident, courageous, free

Loved
affection, connected, empathy, pursued, tenderness, embraced, cherished

Approved
proud, good, accepted, respected, justified, important, valuable

Safe
comforted, relief, trusting, protected, intimate, secure

Hopeful
patient, encouraged, optimistic, wonder, anticipating, eager, believing

Peaceful
comfortable, at rest, relaxed, content, calm, fulfilled, serene

© Tony Stoltzfus 2013 | All Rights Reserved

Desires Wheel

The underlying needs and motivations rooted in my humanness that drive me.

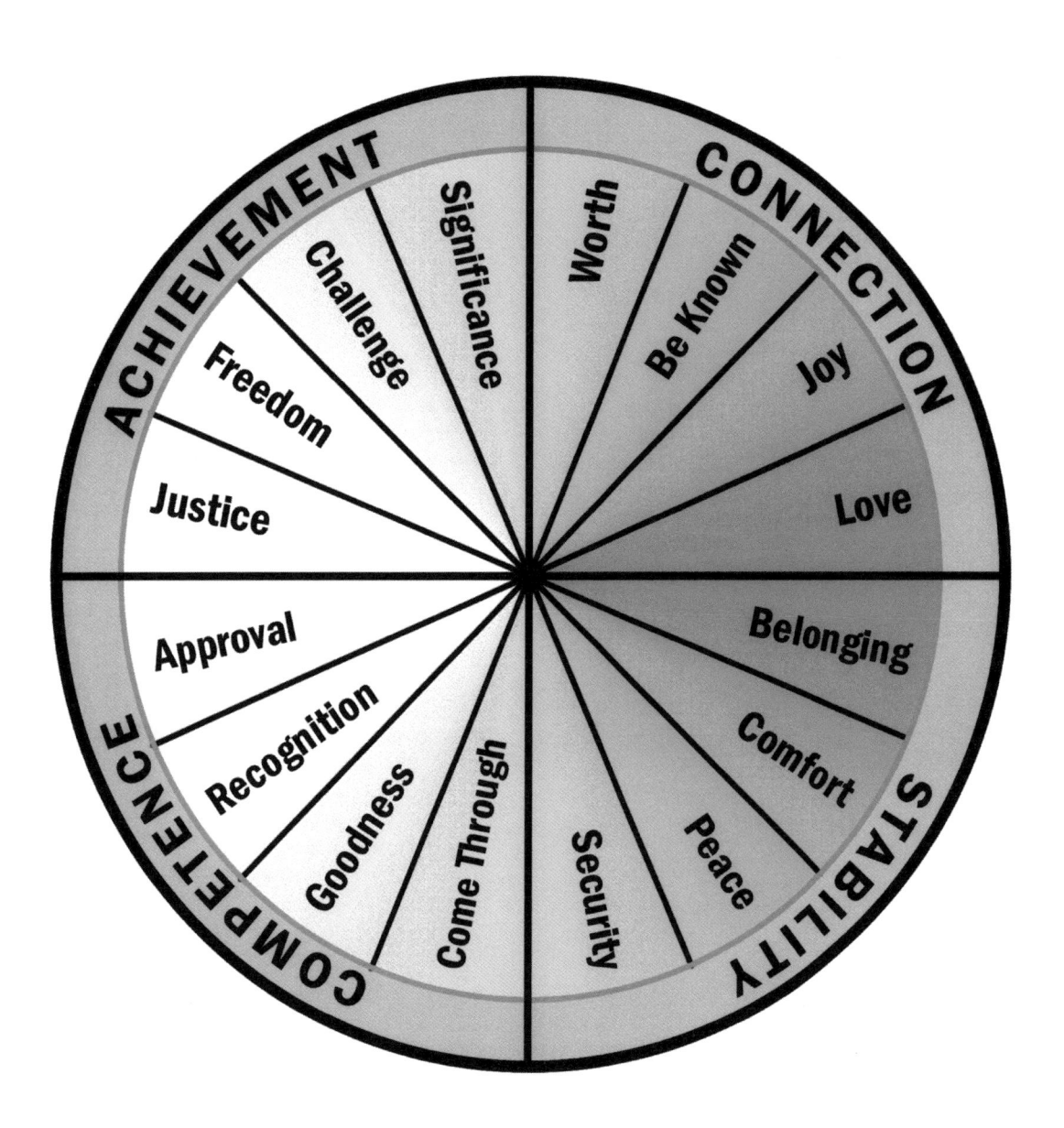

ACHIEVEMENT: Significance, Challenge, Freedom, Justice

CONNECTION: Worth, Be Known, Joy, Love

STABILITY: Belonging, Comfort, Peace, Security

COMPETENCE: Come Through, Goodness, Recognition, Approval

© Tony Stoltzfus 2013 | All Rights Reserved